Short *ish* Walks
The South Devon Coast

Paul White

Bossiney Books · Launceston

The approximate locations of the walks in this book

All the walks in this book were checked prior to printing,
at which time the instructions were correct. However, changes
can occur in the countryside over which neither the author nor
the publishers have any control. Please let us know
if you encounter any serious problems.

First published 2008 by
Bossiney Books Ltd, Langore, Launceston, Cornwall PL15 8LD
www.bossineybooks.com

© 2008 Paul White All rights reserved
ISBN 978-1-899383-96-2

Acknowledgements
The maps are by Graham Hallowell
The photograph on page 31 is by Robert Hesketh
All other photographs are by the author
Cover based on a design by Heards Design Partnership
Printed in Great Britain by R Booth Ltd, Mabe, Cornwall

Introduction

These 'shortish' circular walks range from 5 to 10km (3 1/4 to 6 1/4 miles) and typically take 2 to 3 hours. The exact time will vary according to your fitness, weather conditions (take your time if it is slippery underfoot) and above all how interested you are in what you see. The duration times given make no allowance for this, as it is such a variable.

The area covered is the coast from Turnchapel, on the edge of Plymouth, round to Dartmouth. All the walks involve a section of the coast path with a rural outward journey or return, giving some idea of the countryside which backs this magnificent coast.

The scenery is fantastic, and full of geological interest. In summer, you are likely to see sailing craft in profusion, and you will often have a grandstand view of yacht races.

Comfort and safety

Inland country walking involves some mud at most times of the year, and after heavy rain, a lot of mud! You will also inevitably from time to time encounter farm animals, ill-maintained gates and damaged signposts, but on the whole this area is very walker-friendly.

I strongly recommend walking boots, not just because of the mud but to give ankle support. I also find a walking pole invaluable when descending the steeper parts of the coast path. Cliffs are exposed to the wind, so you may well find you need an extra layer or two, as well as a waterproof. Carry water with you (dehydration makes you tired) and some spare food.

The two obvious hazards are firstly the cliff paths, especially where the coast is eroding. They are unfenced, so children and dogs should be supervised. Secondly, traffic: where lanes are used, they are on the whole quiet, but care is nevertheless needed.

A less obvious hazard is ticks, which can cause Lyme disease. For this reason, and also because inland footpaths may be overgrown with nettles and other vicious vegetation, I strongly recommend you do not walk bare-legged away from the coast path itself.

Whilst I doubt that you will get lost on these walks, our sketch maps only cover the route of the walk itself. The OS Explorer map OL20 (double-sided) covers this whole coast and is excellent value.

Paul White

Walk 1   Bovisand and Turnchapel

Distance: 9.5km (6 miles)   Time: 2¾ hours
Character: A fascinating mixture of views over Plymouth Sound, a
surprisingly rural section, then a generally interesting and attractive
route through waterside areas of the city. Fairly easy walking, apart
from a few flights of steps on the coast path near the start.

Start from the Jennycliff car park (free, SX493524). (Alternatively, there are free car parks at Bovisand and Turnchapel.)

In front of you is a green area, with benches and a café. Turn left across the front of the benches and pick up a beaten path. This is soon identified as the coast path (POOLE 175½ MILES). It winds through woodland, with several short flights of steps, then leads round to Fort Bovisand with its quay. Continue ahead down more steps, cross a footbridge, then turn left up a lane.

At the far end of a car park, bear right on the coast path, HEYBROOK BAY. At the foot of the steps, turn left on a footpath, unsigned. Follow it up the valley, crossing a private drive on the way. Reaching a lane, continue ahead. When the lane reaches a more major road, continue ahead but after just 25 m turn left, then immediately left again up steps (PUBLIC FOOTPATH RADFORD LAKE).

4

Continue in the same direction till you go through a kissing gate into a wood. Keep left, then after 50 m at a waymark post turn *right*. This path descends via steps to a neat suburban area. Cross two streets to a footpath just behind the REDDICLIFF CLOSE sign and zig-zag down. Pass the end of a close and continue down to a T-junction of paths.

Turn left, and follow the Erme-Plym Trail. Within a bit of open ground, the path turns right. Cross the main road and follow ERME-PLYM signs into parkland. Bear right at the kissing gate to walk with the stream, and later the lake, on your left. Turn left across the dam and follow the path around the treatment works. At a fingerpost, turn sharp right for the coast path (acorn sign). Turn right down a street, pass the Royal Oak and follow coast path signs around an inlet, out round the point and past MOD buildings.

It looks unpromising but there is a pedestrian gate at the end leading into Turnchapel village (photograph above) with its attractive late 18th and early 19th century cottages. Turn left at the Clovelly Bay Inn, past a chapel 'restored 1879'. At the top of the hill, turn right through a car park, SOUTH-WEST COAST PATH CLOVELLY BAY. You will reach the Plymouth Yacht Haven, at the neck of the Mount Batten peninsula.

You might want to walk out to the point (views over the Barbican, Citadel and Hoe) but otherwise walk up to the roundabout, cross the road and take the coast path left, which leads back to the start.

Walk 2   Wembury

Distance: 7km (4¹/₂ miles)   Time: 2 hours
(Can be shortened by 1km, cutting out a steep descent and ascent.)
Character: South Devon farmland and coast path, with views over
the Yealm estuary at Warren Point. Could be connected, using the
seasonal ferry, with Walk 3. Apart from the optional visit to the ferry,
fairly easy walking.

Start from the car park at Wembury beach (SX 518485). Walk across
the back of the beach, start on the coast path and after just 20m turn
right, go through a gate and turn right again onto the upper of two
driveways. Continue along this access drive as far as a lane, then turn
right.

  You might well want to explore the National Trust's Mill Field, on
the left. Otherwise, walk past and, at the road junction, turn sharp
left on PUBLIC FOOTPATH AND BRIDLEWAY. The path and bridleway
are separated, with the footpath on the right, which is very welcome
if the ground is muddy. At a lane, turn left then after 50m turn right,
TRAIN ROAD LANGDON. Keep right at a path junction, climb and cross

6

fields, keep right at another junction, then follow the footpath when it bears right across a field.

Reaching a lane, turn right. At the Odd Wheel, turn left. Opposite the shops, turn right into a footpath, BROWNHILL LANE. At a path junction, turn left then shortly right up steps. Follow the well-beaten path past Wembury House, then turn right on a tarmac lane, which later becomes a track, TO FERRY AND COAST PATH. At length this leads to a gate, by the old rocket house, where you have a choice of turning right immediately (in which case, skip the next paragraph) or walking down to the ferry. And back up! There are good views on the way.

A gentle descent down the track leads to cottages and the ferry, which is seasonal and has varying hours, so check return times if using it. You can either return up the same track, or, just 5m beyond the ferry access, turn left up a footpath – there are steps which zigzag up, so it is considerably more demanding than the track. Either way will bring you back to the rocket house.

Then take the coast path, WEMBURY. Just before Wembury church, turn left, LINK TO CAR PARK.

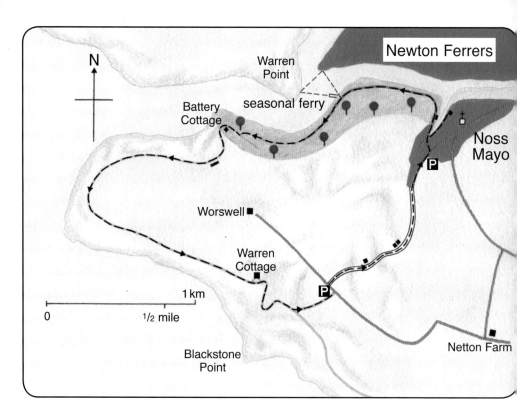

Walk 3   Noss Mayo

Distance: 7km (4 1/2 miles)   Time: 2 hours
Character: An easy walk, with gentle gradients but a great variety of
scenery, from open farmland at the start, down to the creekside village
of Noss Mayo, along the wooded creekside, then a stretch of coast path
on National Trust land.

   Noss has a famously picturesque setting, and like its neighbour
across the creek, Newton Ferrers, has gone up and up in the world's
(and especially estate agents') estimation. A century of development,
especially in Newton, and in recent decades the growth of second home
and boat ownership, have made them ideal places for the well-keeled.

Start from the National Trust's Warren car park. (To get there, follow signs to Noss Mayo. Keep left up to the church. At the church,
keep left again. Take a right turning for NETTON and WORSWELL. Pass
Netton Farm and turn right, WORSWELL.)

   From the car park, turn left along the lane and then almost immediately right, PUBLIC FOOTPATH NOSS MAYO. This is mostly a broad stony

8

track and leads into the village past tennis courts and a car park. Bear left just beyond the bus turning area, down to the village hall and the Tilly Institute.

You might like to divert briefly right along Creekside Road for views, and the Swan Inn. Then return to the Tilly Institute and turn right, this time past the Ship Inn. Follow the creekside lane, passing the landing stage of the triangular ferry service to Wembury and Newton Ferrers.

Keep right at a fork, COAST PATH STOKE. Then bear right on COAST PATH, briefly a footpath then joining a track. A notice explains its origin as Lord Revelstoke's Drive. Follow the coast path for 2 km, to Warren Cottage. After that, the path snakes about a bit, then forks. Take the left fork, signed for the car park.

Lord Revelstoke

Edward Baring (1828-1897), First Baron Revelstoke, was a third-generation merchant banker who did everything on the grand scale, including buying the 1600 hectare Membland Estate.

His financial dealings were utterly reckless, and Barings had to be rescued by a Bank of England loan. Revelstoke was disgraced and his personal assets were sold, but his son turned the disaster around and the bank remained solvent.

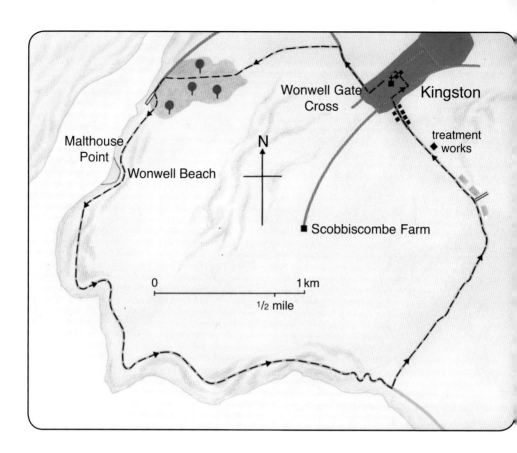

Walk 4   Kingston and the Erme estuary

Distance: 8.5km (5¹/₄ miles)   Time: 2³/₄ hours
Character: Attractive inland and coastal scenery, relatively easy
walking throughout except for one steep descent. A short stretch of
quiet lane, then footpaths and bridleways throughout. If you consider
combining this walk with Walk 5, be aware that the intervening coast
path section involves very steep ascents and descents.

There is usually parking at Kingston near the church (SX635478).
Starting from the Dolphin Inn, turn left past the church and walk
up to Wonwell Gate Cross. Turn right along a lane. After 400m turn
left, FOOTPATH WONWELL BEACH. This crosses fields then descends
through a wood.

   Reaching a lane, turn left. Just after it becomes a track, turn left,
COAST PATH BIGBURY-ON-SEA. The path initially runs beside the estuary, with attractive views inland, then turns left along the coast.

By coast path standards it is not too hilly and makes for steady walking. Pass through a wicket gate beside a large concrete cattle trough, and climb to Hoist Point, where there is a granite bench. Continue along the path, which suddenly descends steeply.

At the foot, just before a wooden footbridge with a notice about a permissive path, turn left inland. The path crosses a stream then passes through a wood. At a junction, bear right PUBLIC BRIDLEWAY KINGSTON. Pass a series of pools on your right, continuing up the left side of the valley. These are in fact downstream from a treatment works, but when I walked this way there were no unpleasant odours.

After gently gaining height over a distance of more than 2 km (would that all uphill paths were as gentle!) the bridleway arrives at the edge of Kingston and becomes a lane. Follow this up to a T-junction.

Turn right, then first left and you will find the sixteenth-century Dolphin Inn on either side of the road.

Walk 5   Ringmore and Bigbury

*Distance: 8km (5 miles) but can be shortened   Time: 2¹/₂ hours
Character: Attractive countryside and coastal walking, mainly on
footpaths but with one 550m section of lane (used by the Coast
Path) into Bigbury, which can be busy. Several moderate ascents and
descents. The optional visit to Ayrmer Cove involves a steep descent.*

Start from the National Trust Ayrmer Cove car park at Ringmore
(SX650456), contributions requested. Leave by the AYRMER COVE exit.
After 100m, turn right VILLAGE and JOURNEY'S END. Follow a path, then
a lane. At a T-junction, to explore the village and locate the Journey's
End pub, turn left, but for the walk turn right.

At a T-junction turn left past Challaborough Cottages. Pass Cross
Manor and turn right into a lane, signed as a dead end. At the end, take
the PUBLIC FOOTPATH, then continue in the same direction, PUBLIC
FOOTPATH, to cross the valley. Descend to a track, take the kissing gate
nearly opposite (waymarked) and follow the path across a stream and
up the other side. Cross a lane and then another valley.

Reaching a ridge, continue ahead COCKLERIDGE. On reaching the
road at Mount Folly Farm, turn left and after 50m turn right, PUBLIC
FOOTPATH. (You could omit the visit to Cockleridge, saving some distance and one ascent, but you would miss some lovely views over to
Bantham and down the Avon estuary to Burgh Island.)

Keep the hedge on your right to the end of the field, and cross a stile into a golf course. Continue till you reach a tarmac drive, then turn right, PUBLIC FOOTPATH COCKLERIDGE. Where indicated, turn left through a gate. Keep the hedge on your left round two sides of a field and continue down to the shore of the estuary. Turn right BIGBURY-ON-SEA and follow the path back up to Mount Folly.

Turn left down the road, which forms part of the Coast Path. It can be busy in season, so take care. Walk on the right to face the oncoming traffic. After 550 m, turn left onto a footpath with an acorn waymark. This winds down to the beach, and a further diversion from the road (signed COAST PATH) will bring you to a massive car park, where there are toilets, a café, a shop, and the possibility of visiting Burgh Island.

The coast path follows the lane past the car park, then through an overspill car park, then briefly a lane, COAST PATH CHALLABOROUGH, then a path. Pass the Challaborough Bay Holiday Park, turn left at Slipway Cottage, walk past the recycling bank and bear right to join COAST PATH AYRMER COVE. At a junction of paths, you have a choice. Either turn right, RINGMORE, along a near-level path to the car park, or, if you still have a bit of spare energy, continue on the coast path.

Descend steeply to Ayrmer Bay, a lovely spot beautifully maintained by the National Trust, then turn right up the valley (PUBLIC BRIDLEWAY RINGMORE) along Smugglers' Lane. This climbs gently. At the top, turn right for the car park or straight on for the Journey's End.

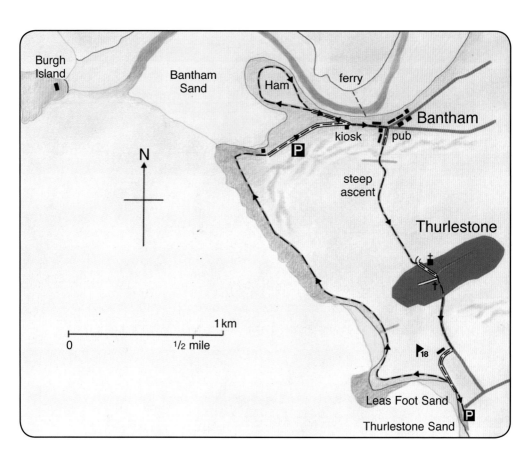

Walk 6   Thurlestone and Bantham

Distance: 7.5km (4¹/₂ miles)   Time: 2 hours
Character: A popular walk along the cliff path with wonderful views
of Burgh Island and the coast, then an exploration of an area of dune
and beach. You could equally start from the Bantham beach car park.
One steep ascent, but mostly easy walking on well trodden paths.

Start from the car park at the north end of Thurlestone Sand
(SX 676420). Facing the sea, turn right along COAST PATH PUBLIC
BRIDLEWAY. Follow the path when it diverts along the cliff top, and
continue along it to Bantham Sand.

When the tide is out, you can take a short cut across the beach to
Bantham Ham. Otherwise, follow COAST PATH TO FERRY through the
beach car park. At the ticket kiosk at the entrance to the car park, turn
sharp left to explore the dune area.

14

If you omit the exploration of the dune area, you will cut the total walk distance by 1.6 km, a mile.

From the ticket kiosk, continue up the lane to the Sloop Inn, bear right then immediately turn right beside the inn, PUBLIC FOOTPATH THURLESTONE. At the foot of a slope, turn left, cut across the field and turn right on a well-beaten path up a steep hill. (May I recommend the view to your right, best seen from about two thirds of the way up, and well worth stopping for!)

Follow yellow waymarks to Thurlestone. Pass the church on your left. At the war memorial and village green, continue ahead down the lane, past tennis courts. Turn right on a driveway past the Golf Club and then retrace your steps to the car park.

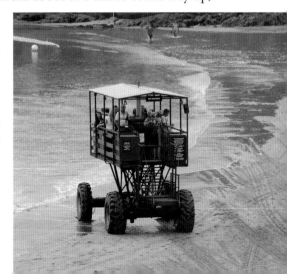

Right: The unique Burgh Island sea tractor works at high tide

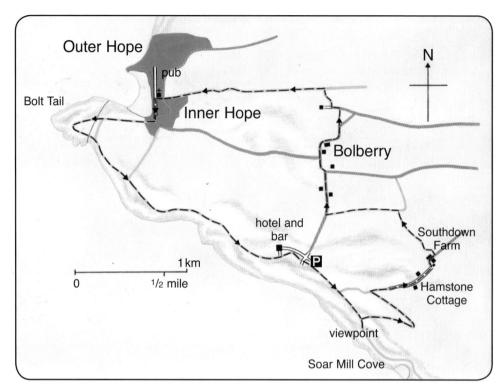

Walk 7   Bolberry and Hope Cove

Distance: 10.25 km (6¼ miles) Time: 3¼ hours
(Could be cut to 6.5 km by walking up the lane from the car park.)
*Character: A lovely mix of farmland and coast, visiting the old fishing
village of Inner Hope and the prehistoric promontory fort on Bolt Tail,
which may have sheltered the locals in time of war, or perhaps been a
trading post for foreign merchants. One steep descent near the start,
but the ascents are gentle to moderate. Could be combined with Walk
8 to make an all-day walk.*

Start from the National Trust Bolberry Down car park (SX690385).
Facing the sea, turn left through the car park and pick up the coast
path. At the sign indicating CATHOLE CLIFF, carry on for 100 m for
the view, then retrace your steps to the sign and take the path inland,
descending steeply. The path may be a little overgrown and muddy at
some times of year. At the foot, turn left into South Down Farm and
follow the beaten path gently uphill through fields to a T-junction.

Turn right, MALBOROUGH. The track leads up to and through Southdown Farm, which has been developed for National Trust holiday

16

accommodation. Leaving the farm, turn left, PUBLIC FOOTPATH and follow the yellow waymarks and footpath signs round the farm buildings and along the side of a field. At the end of the field, cross a stile and turn left, JACOBS LANE BOLBERRY DOWN.

On reaching a lane, turn right. At the T-junction turn left, HOPE COVE. Take special care round the bend. At the next junction bear right downhill. Climb a slope and continue ahead, SWEETHEARTS LANE. Turn left at a T-junction and after 80 m (after passing through a gate signed 'Higher Barton') turn right up four steps, PUBLIC FOOT-PATH GALMPTON, and follow waymarks.

At the field at the end of the path, turn right. Go through a metal gate and then turn left at a waymark post. This broad track continues in roughly the same direction for 1.25 km, then becomes a lane. Cross a road (or turn right for the Hope & Anchor pub) into the footpath past St Clements church, then turn left onto the coast path.

Cross behind the beach (diverting left if you want to explore Inner Hope) then take the steps beside the lifeboat house (COAST PATH SALCOMBE). The path leads up to the entrance of the Bolt Tail promontory fort.

Climb to the highest point to enjoy the views, then turn and follow the path with the sea on your right. After about 2.5 km you will reach the Bolberry Down car park.

Walk 8   Soar Mill Cove

Distance: 5km (3 miles) Time: 1½ hours
Character: A short walk but with lovely cliff scenery and a delightful
sandy cove to visit. Mostly footpaths with one short section of narrow
lane giving access to the beach and a hotel. One steep descent. Could
be combined with either Walk 7 or Walk 9.

Start from the National Trust car park at East Soar (SX713375). To
get there, head towards Salcombe on A381. At Malborough, turn right
GALMPTON BOLBERRY SOAR. Just past the church, keep left, BOLBERRY
SOAR, then follow signs for SOAR then for EAST SOAR FARM. At a crossing, by former coastguard houses, continue ahead to the car park.

   From the car park take the track which is a continuation of the lane
by which you arrived. After 100m, turn right PUBLIC FOOTPATH LINK
TO THE COAST PATH. Pass through the grounds of newly restored
Middle Soar and continue on PUBLIC FOOTPATH. At a path crossing,
continue ahead, acorn waymark.

   A gate leads out on to the cliffs. Turn right SOAR MILL COVE. A

18

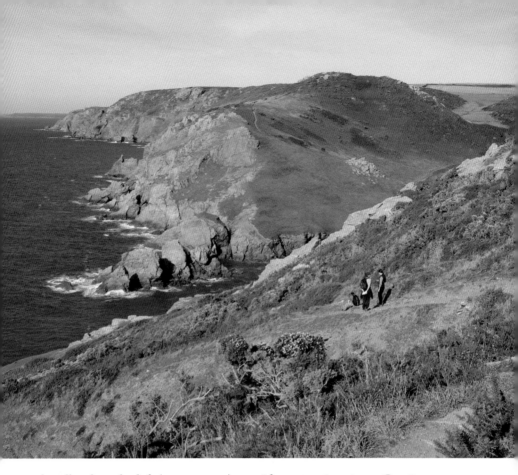

headland on the left (GOAT ROCK) provides extensive views. Continue along the coast path until it descends to sandy Soar Mill Cove.

To link with Walk 7, turn left BOLBERRY BOLT TAIL then at the next junction fork right (LOWER PATH TO BOLBERRY) and continue up the valley to the signed entrance into Southdown Farm.

Otherwise, turn right for HIGHER SOAR MALBOROUGH and ascend steadily. The well concealed buildings of Soar Mill Cove Hotel come into view. Keep to the left of them and join a lane. Pass the beach car park (you could start here but it looked expensive) and then Lower Soar, with its attractive thatched 'Olde Cottage'.

At a mind-blowingly complex road layout – not so much a Spaghetti, more of a Vermicelli Junction, which had a motorist utterly confused even as I walked past – do the simple thing and turn right onto PUBLIC FOOTPATH MIDDLE SOAR LINK TO COAST PATH. Now follow the well waymarked path through fields back to the car park.

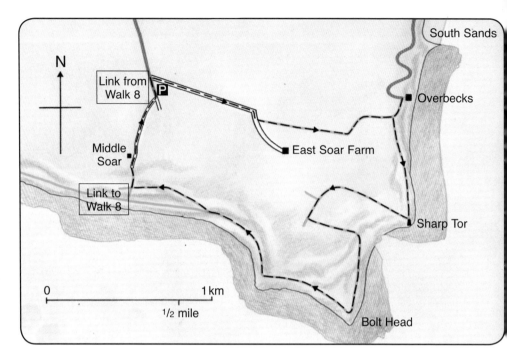

Walk 9 Overbecks and Bolt Head

Distance: 7km (4¹/₄ miles) Time: 2 hours
Character: Stunning views of coast and estuary. Mainly easy walking,
though with a couple of moderate ascents. Could be combined with
Walk 8.

Start from the National Trust car park at East Soar (SX713375). See
Walk 8 for directions for getting to this car park.

From the car park, take the track signed SALCOMBE OVERBECKS
SHARPTOR. Soar was, you might think appropriately from its name, a
wartime airfield, RAF Bolt Head. It still has a landing strip. According
to the 1946 one-inch OS map, however, the farms were then called
Sewer, not Soar, and there was a Sewer Mill Sand where now there is
Soar Mill Cove. By what process, I wonder, were the historic names
changed? Certainly it is an improvement!

The track turns right. Shortly after, turn left for OVERBECKS, across
fields. At a fingerpost, turn left, OVERBECKS, going through two gates
to walk with the fence on your left. Then shortly turn right, OVERBECKS.
At the next junction either carry straight on to visit the National Trust
house and garden at Overbecks, or turn right SHARP TOR STARE HOLE
BOLT HEAD.

Views of the estuary open up, especially from Sharp Tor. The path then winds down, to cross a stream. Go through the gate and turn left down the slope. Turn right at the foot, and climb, rounding Bolt Head. At the top of the next slope, continue ahead, SOAR MILL COVE.

Reaching another junction, turn right, MIDDLE SOAR SOAR MILL COVE (unless you want to link with Walk 8, in which case you should continue along the cliff path).

Keep the field wall on your right till you reach a path crossing, then turn right MALBOROUGH. Pass to the right of Middle Soar and continue up the access track till you reach a tarmac lane. Turn left back to the start.

Overbecks

This National Trust property has a microclimate perfectly suiting the rare and exotic species in its garden, which can be enjoyed against spectacular background views. The house contains the idiosyncratic collections of the former owner, chemist Otto Overbeck (1860-1937) and also a tearoom. House and tearoom are open seasonally, but the garden is open most days of the year.

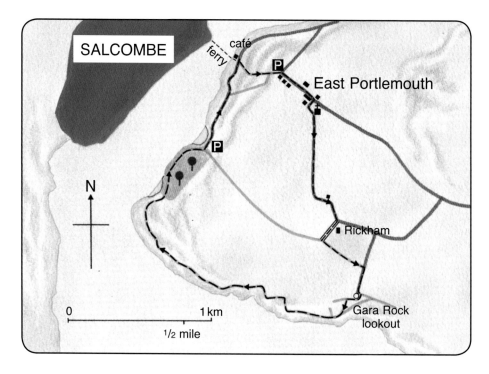

Walk 10   East Portlemouth

Distance: 6km (3³/₄ miles)   Time: 1³/₄ hours
Character: A short inland stretch on very quiet lanes leads to the coast
path at Gara Rock. The path provides lovely views as you approach
Salcombe Harbour. It is uneven at one point, where it runs near the
cliff, and vertigo sufferers might have a problem with it. There is also
one steep ascent, from the ferry to the village.

The passenger ferry from Salcombe, which operates in the summer
months, would make an ideal start for this walk – but do check the
time of the last return ferry of the day.

If arriving by car in East Portlemouth, there is a parking area
downhill from the church, at the top of 'Passageway', which is the
bridleway between the village and the ferry.

From the parking area, walk uphill to the church, and turn right on
the lane to RICKHAM. Turn right down the NO THROUGH ROAD and
follow the track up into the trees, then turn left (yellow waymark)
onto a path. After crossing two fields, cross a track and go through
the gate opposite, then turn right down a lane.

(At the time of writing, the hotel at the end of this lane had been

22

demolished but the new development had not been started, so please be prepared for minor variations and footpath diversions.)

At the end of the lane is the Gara Rock lookout. Turn briefly left, then after 20m right, PUBLIC FOOTPATH MILLBAY. Keep left at a fork, then right at the waymark to join the coast path. Follow it round to a National Trust car park (busy in season, so not a good place to start the walk). From this point a narrow lane leads ahead, to the ferry, where the Venus café provides refreshment for waiting passengers.

Turn inland almost opposite the café up PUBLIC BRIDLEWAY EAST PORTLEMOUTH. At a junction, continue ahead, EAST PORTLEMOUTH VILLAGE.

Walk 11   East Prawle

Distance: 8.75km (5½ miles)   Time: 3 hours
Character: A classic blend of beautiful coast and South Hams
farmland. Whilst much of the walk is easy, there are two steep ascents,
and a couple of places where the coast path is uneven and rocky,
running near the cliff edge – we think it unsuitable for dogs. The walk
can also be quite muddy in places.

The remote village of East Prawle has a free village parking area
around a green (SX 781364) and supports two pubs and a café, not to
mention public toilets. BUT the parking area can be busy, especially
at weekends.

From the parking area, walk down the SINGLE TRACK ROAD WITH
PASSING PLACES, also signed for walkers PRAWLE POINT. Where the
lane turns left, continue ahead PUBLIC BRIDLEWAY. After 1.25km,
turn left at a T-junction, down towards Elender Cove (see photograph
opposite), one of the most beautiful on this stretch of coast.

Keep left at the next waymarked path junction, round the head of
a small valley, then turn right down to the coast path – the descent
is steep and may be slippery if wet. Turn left along the coast path.

24

Initially deceptively easy, the following few hundred metres are really difficult going, climbing over rocks. But it will get easier later! When you reach the National Coastwatch lookout post at Prawle Point (Devon's most southerly point) turn left to pass in front of a terrace of houses. Now continue along the coast path for 2 km.

When you reach a field where the path doubles back on itself, continue round to the fingerpost and then turn right, COAST PATH LANNACOMBE. After you pass Maelcombe House, the craggy cliffs get ever closer and ever more bizarre. You will again need to watch your step since the path becomes rocky and uneven as it rounds Woodcombe Point.

At the Woodcombe Sand waymark, continue ahead and at the next junction keep left, uphill, WOODCOMBE. The path is both steep and at times muddy. At a T-junction of paths, turn left, PUBLIC BRIDLEWAY EAST PRAWLE. Join a track, follow it round a right turn, then turn left, PUBLIC BRIDLEWAY EAST PRAWLE.

Ignore a blue waymarked turn and follow the track, later a lane, to a T-junction within the village. Turn left and follow a lane which wriggles around past property entrances, to a T-junction. Turn left, then first right, back to the start.

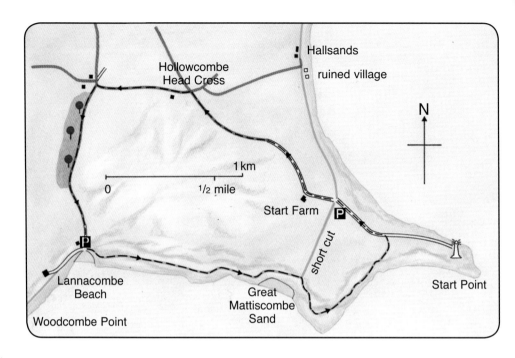

Walk 12 Start Point

Distance: 6.5km (4 miles) Time: 2 hours
Character: An easy walk which gets better and better as it proceeds.
After a modest start, it descends into a lovely valley, then heads out to
the coast path for some remarkable cliff scenery. There is more tarmac
than in most of our walks, but the lanes are quiet and very attractive.

The coast path from Lannacombe to Great Mattiscombe Sand is
easy walking. From there to Start Point is uneven but there is an easy
short cut which avoids this section. There are possible short extensions
in either direction, both with fairly easy walking. This walk could be
combined with either Walk 11 or Walk 13 to make a full day's walking.

There are several tempting beaches on this walk, so if tide and
temperature are suitable, go prepared.

Park at the Start Point car park (SX821375). Begin by walking back
along the access drive, past Start Farm and the radio masts, and then
continue to Hollowcombe Head Cross. Turn left, LANNACOMBE, and
descend to a road junction. Take the first left, LANNACOMBE, and walk
seaward to Lannacombe Beach.

You might want to divert right for a closer look at the remarkable
rocky outcrops on Woodcombe Point, for comparison with Start

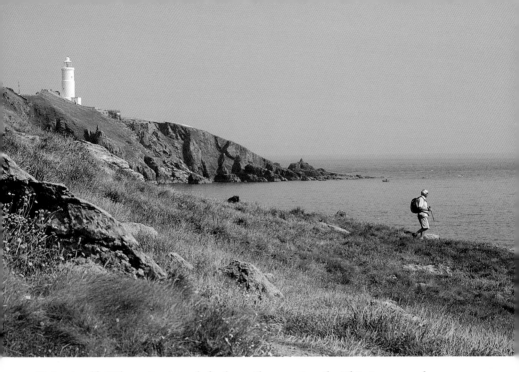

Point itself. Otherwise turn left along the coast path. This is an eroding coast, so please take notice of warning signs and diversions. At a path junction, you could take the left turn back to the car park, or turn right, START POINT. This section of the coast path does need care and is not recommended to vertigo sufferers.

Nearing Start Point, the path climbs to the crest of the ridge. Just over the top is the lighthouse access drive, and you could divert down to the lighthouse which is 500m away. Otherwise, turn left up the tarmac driveway which leads to the car park.

Hallsands is about 1km (2/3 mile) away down the coast path to the north – a gentle descent and easy walking.

Hallsands in the nineteenth century was a fishing village with 37 houses, protected from the sea by a pebble beach. When, in the 1890s, the Admiralty wanted to expand Plymouth's dockyards, they gave permission for the shingle to be dredged. Despite protests, the dredging went ahead. By 1900 damage to the village was evident, but dredging continued. In 1917 storms destroyed all but one of the houses. The compensation offered to the homeless villagers collectively was just £6000.

Walk 13   Beesands and Hallsands

Distance: 9km (5¹/₂ miles)   Time: 2³/₄ hours
Character: A contrast of coast and countryside – shingle beaches at
Beesands and Hallsands, undemanding coast path between – and
on the inland route both farmland and the outskirts of a landscaped
estate. Some footpaths may be a bit overgrown, so bare legs could be a
real liability.

Start from Beesands, where there is normally plenty of parking. (Alternatively, you could start from Hallsands.) Facing the sea, turn left (north) along the back of the beach and past a lake. At the end of the beach access track, turn left to pass behind a substantial white house, then turn left again, PUBLIC FOOTPATH TO WIDEWELL.

Climb a stile into a large field. Keep the hedge on your left to the very end of the field, then turn right as signed (PUBLIC FOOTPATH) and cross two stiles into woodland. Keep right past houses, then continue on a private drive signed PUBLIC FOOTPATH.

After a further 250m, turn left, PUBLIC FOOTPATH BEESON. Follow waymarks. Emerging from the grounds of Widdicombe House, descend a field with a wall on your left. Go through a wooden gate at the bottom of the field, then follow PUBLIC FOOTPATH almost straight ahead, passing to the left of Lower Widdicombe Farm. Faced with two gates, take the one on the right.

28

Cross the valley bottom, join a track, bear right and you will arrive in Beeson. Continue ahead to a T-junction and turn left, BEESANDS, then after 100 m (by 'Camps End' and 'Rose Cottage') turn right up a minor lane. Climb steadily to a T-junction. Turn left and then at Huckham Barn Cross continue ahead, FARM ONLY.

Reaching the farm gate, turn left down a footpath. Go through a gate beside barns, following red arrow waymarks, then through an unusually wide wooden gate into a footpath. Follow this down to a track. Ignore the footpath sign for Hallsands but take the track to a lane. Turn left, then after 200 m turn right, BRIDLEWAY LANE BICKERTON. In Bickerton, bear right (see map) for Bickerton Farm, snaking down, then following PUBLIC FOOTPATH HALLSANDS. Turn left (PUBLIC FOOTPATH) when faced with a glass-fronted house. The track becomes a path, then emerges into a field. Keep the hedge, later a fence, on your left to the very end of the field. Cross a stile and turn left onto a lane.

At the top, after a diversion to the viewing platform for the ruined village, continue along the lane, which becomes a path. Go across the back of the beach and follow the coast path for BEESANDS.

At a junction, bear right (acorn waymark) back down to Beesands.

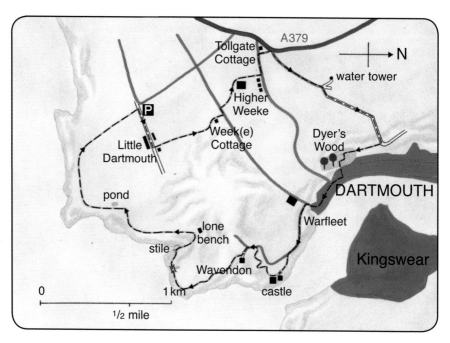

Walk 14   Around Dartmouth

Distance: 8.3 km (5¼ miles)   Time: 2½ hours
Character: Initially quiet countryside, then wonderful views over the
Dart estuary, and finally a dramatic stretch of coastline. Several ascents
and descents steep enough for steps – and benches – to be provided.

Park at the NT car park at Little Dartmouth (SX 874491). With the coast
at your back, turn right onto the PUBLIC BRIDLEWAY. Walk through
Little Dartmouth farmyard and look out for a signpost on the
left. Turn left and head for WEEK COTTAGE. Descend a hill, go through
a gate to the left of Weeke Cottage and turn left when you reach the
lane. After 50m turn right (PUBLIC FOOTPATH SWANNATON).

At a triple junction take the middle track, with a yellow waymark, and
walk quietly past someone's living room to pick up the track again. Walk
up a field to a lane and turn left. After 220 m, turn right past Tollgate
Cottage (with its radio masts). Turn right onto the busy A379 for just
25m before keeping right onto the straight lane ahead – quiet except
on a Sunday, when the recycling centre is open and care is needed.

Just before you reach a tall water tower, turn right on a tarmac track
with a red circle sign, and head downhill, towards the River Dart.
After about 700 m, where the track takes a sharp left turn, turn right,
PUBLIC FOOTPATH DYERS WOOD. Take the upper path when it forks.

Continue into Dyers Wood, crossing a stile and taking the path ahead. Then turn left down a flight of wooden-edged steps, which wind steeply down to a road – take care, they can be slippery. Cross and descend the flight of concrete steps opposite, down to a lower road. Turn right, then continue ahead into Warfleet Road. Turn left for DARTMOUTH CASTLE and cross a creek. Keep left, and walk to the church and castle. Walk through to the tearooms and car park.

Now pick up the COAST PATH for LITTLE DARTMOUTH. You will notice its acorn waymarks all the way back to the car park, but there are a few unmarked junctions. The steps eventually wind and climb up to a road. Turn left, then immediately bear left. Continue on the path. Pass to the right of 'Wavendon'.

Continue along the coast path, which emerges into the open at Blackstone Point, then hugs the open coast. When the tide is in and the sea rough this is very dramatic; in extreme weather conditions it would require caution. Immediately after crossing a footbridge, turn right inland and walk up as far as a stile on the right. Take the coast path inland, over the stile and up a broad, very steep, grassy track to a lone bench, at which point the path turns sharply to the left.

A short distance beyond a gate, the path forks. Keep left. In time you will reach a small pond. The path continues ahead to a field gate on the horizon. At the gate, turn right, and follow the broad grassy path, keeping a wall and then a fence to your right. When you reach a kissing gate, go through and follow the path uphill, back to your car.

Tourist Information Centres

Ashburton 01364 653426	Plymouth 01752 304849
Dartmouth 01803 834224	Salcombe 01548 843927
Kingsbridge 01548 853195	Totnes 01803 863168

Some other Bossiney walks books

Shortish walks on Dartmoor
Shortish walks on Exmoor
Shortish walks – East Devon
Shortish walks – North Devon
Shortish walks – Torbay and Dartmouth
Shortish walks – Bodmin Moor

Really short walks – North Dartmoor
Really short walks – South Dartmoor
North Dartmoor pub walks
South Dartmoor pub walks

Three other Bossiney books which might add to your interest in the walks are all by local author Robert Hesketh:

Devon's Geology – an introduction
Devon's Smugglers – the truth behind the fiction
Dartmouth, a Shortish Guide.